JENETH UGWU

At the Crossroads of Fate

Copyright © 2025 by Jeneth Ugwu

All rights reserved. No part of this publication may be reproduced, stored or transmitted in any form or by any means, electronic, mechanical, photocopying, recording, scanning, or otherwise without written permission from the publisher. It is illegal to copy this book, post it to a website, or distribute it by any other means without permission.

Jeneth Ugwu asserts the moral right to be identified as the author of this work.

Jeneth Ugwu has no responsibility for the persistence or accuracy of URLs for external or third-party Internet Websites referred to in this publication and does not guarantee that any content on such Websites is, or will remain, accurate or appropriate.

First edition

This book was professionally typeset on Reedsy.
Find out more at reedsy.com

Contents

1	The Unseen Crossroad	1
2	The Silent Pursuit	5
3	The Invisible Threads	9
4	The Hollow Silence	13
5	The Unseen Path	17
6	Echoes of the Past	21
7	The Hollow Sound	25
8	The Weight of Shadows	29
9	The Hollow Echo	33
10	Beneath the Surface	37
11	The Edge of Silence	41
12	Beneath the Veil	45

1

The Unseen Crossroad

Elliot Stone had always prided himself on his ability to anticipate. As a high-powered corporate strategist, he was known for making decisions with precision, calculating every risk, and forecasting every possible outcome. But that evening, as the sharp wind rattled against the windows of his downtown apartment, Elliot had the unnerving feeling that for the first time in his life, something had escaped his notice.

The letter had arrived earlier that day, tucked into the usual pile of envelopes and bills. At first glance, it appeared ordinary—nothing to warrant a second glance. The handwriting on the envelope was elegant, looping in a way that seemed too deliberate to be casual, yet too personal to be professional. It was addressed to him by name, and the only marking on the back was a wax seal, the image of an ornate compass.

Curiosity had gnawed at him since he saw it. He'd left the letter untouched on the kitchen counter for hours, an object he couldn't quite bring himself to open. He was used to control, to plans, to systems, yet something about the letter felt different—dangerous, even. But now, with the evening stretching into the night, there was no turning back. He had to know.

Sitting on the edge of his polished dining table, Elliot held the letter up to the light. The wax seal caught the faint glow of the lamp beside him, casting shadows over the delicate ridges of the embossed compass. He hesitated, then slid his finger under the flap, tearing it open with a swift motion. A thin slip of paper slipped out, its texture fine, almost like parchment, but with a certain weight to it.

The words were simple, written in the same careful script that adorned the envelope:

"The choice you face is no longer a matter of want. It is a matter of need. The path ahead is only known to those who can see beyond the surface. Look closely at what is about to unfold, and choose wisely. The future you desire, and the one you fear, are both within your grasp. Do not take the wrong turn."

Elliot's pulse quickened as he read the words again. What was this? Some kind of twisted game? The vague, foreboding tone of the message settled over him like a heavy fog. There was nothing in his life that had prepared him for something like this—no boardroom negotiation, no late-night strategy session, no calculated risk could explain the surge of unease rising in his chest.

He glanced around his apartment, as if searching for some sign that he was still grounded in reality. The sleek, modern furnishings, the warm glow of the fireplace, the quiet hum of the city streets below—everything appeared normal, but the letter had already disturbed that normality. It was as if the walls themselves were closing in on him.

He picked up his phone, his fingers trembling slightly, and dialed Olivia. She had been his closest confidante for years, and if anyone could make sense of this, it was her. The phone rang three times before her voice answered, cool but familiar.

"Elliot," she said, "I wasn't expecting to hear from you tonight. Everything okay?"

"I—" Elliot hesitated, gripping the letter tighter. "I don't know. I just received something strange. I'm not sure what to make of it."

"Strange how?" she asked, her tone instantly shifting to something more guarded.

He relayed the message, watching his own words fall into the space between them. When he finished, there was a long pause on the other end of the line.

"You need to be careful," Olivia finally said, her voice low. "I don't know exactly what this is about, but I've heard whispers. There are people who... watch, who know things before they happen."

"Olivia, you're not making any sense," Elliot shot back, his patience starting to fray. "This isn't some conspiracy theory."

"I'm not saying it is," she replied quickly, but with a strange urgency. "Just... keep your eyes open. Trust no one."

Before Elliot could respond, the line went dead. He stared at the phone, the silence in his apartment swallowing him whole. His breath quickened, and for the first time in years, he questioned the very foundations of his existence. Who was watching him? What had Olivia meant by 'trust no one'?

With the phone still pressed to his ear, Elliot's gaze drifted back to the letter, still lying on the table in front of him. There was no going back. Whatever it was—whatever this decision was—it had already begun.

A knock at the door shattered his thoughts.

It was brief—two sharp raps. The kind of knock that belonged to someone who knew what they wanted, but wasn't willing to wait. Elliot stiffened, his heart hammering in his chest. He wasn't expecting anyone. Not at this hour. He rose from the table slowly, his mind racing with the possibilities.

Taking a deep breath, he crossed the room to the door, his hand hovering just above the doorknob. Should he open it? Should he take that first step toward whatever waited on the other side?

The knock came again. Louder this time. More insistent.

With a calm he didn't feel, Elliot twisted the knob and pulled the door open. Nothing.

Just the empty hallway outside his apartment, lit by the dim glow of the building's overhead lights. No one in sight. Yet something caught his eye—a small, folded note, left on the floor just beyond the door. He bent down, his pulse quickening.

The note was identical to the one he had received earlier, but there was one crucial difference: it was marked with a single, unmistakable symbol.

The compass.

And below it, in fresh ink, the words:

"The choice is now yours, and time is running out."
Elliot stood frozen, the weight of the decision pressing down on him.

2

The Silent Pursuit

Elliot couldn't shake the feeling that something had been set in motion. The letter, the knock at the door, the eerie silence that had followed—it was as if he was being drawn into a game he never agreed to play. He couldn't even remember when it had begun, but now, he could feel it deep in his bones: the weight of a decision that was too important to ignore.

The compass symbol had burned itself into his mind. A symbol of direction, of guidance, but also of paths that diverged. And what was he supposed to make of the phrase "time is running out"? The words seemed to echo through his thoughts as he moved through his apartment, his mind too heavy with questions to focus on anything else.

His phone buzzed again, breaking the stillness, but this time, it was an unknown number. He hesitated for a moment before answering, wondering if it was Olivia or someone else trying to warn him. His voice came out more strained than he intended.

"Hello?"

There was a slight pause on the other end before a voice he didn't recognize spoke.

"You've started, haven't you?" The voice was calm, almost conversational, but there was an undercurrent of tension in its tone.

"Who is this?" Elliot demanded, his grip tightening around the phone. The voice was familiar, but he couldn't place it.

"You won't remember me," the voice continued, as if undeterred by his question. "But I've been watching. I've been waiting for this moment."

Elliot's pulse quickened. The sense of being hunted, of being a part of something much larger than himself, was beginning to suffocate him. He scanned the room, as if expecting someone to materialize from the shadows.

"What do you want?" he asked, his voice low but firm.

The voice chuckled, a sound that sent a chill crawling up Elliot's spine. "It's not about what I want. It's about what you want, Mr. Stone. What *you* are willing to risk."

"I don't have time for this," Elliot shot back, trying to keep his composure. "If this is some kind of joke, I—"

"No joke," the voice interrupted. "You'll see soon enough. You'll understand once you choose. But understand this, Elliot: the path ahead isn't one you can just walk away from. It's a decision that will change everything. Your life, your future—it all hinges on what you decide."

Before Elliot could respond, the line went dead. He stared at the phone, his chest tight, his thoughts racing. Who was this person? What was happening to him?

He paced the length of his apartment, trying to make sense of it all. He had no answers. The questions kept coming, piling up in his mind, demanding resolution. And then there was the letter—the second one he'd found at his door—its cryptic warning hanging over him like a sword.

With a deep breath, Elliot walked to the window, his hands resting against the cool glass. He looked out over the city, its lights twinkling like a thousand small promises, and felt the weight of the world pressing down on him. There was no escaping whatever this was. Not anymore.

He turned back to the table, where the two letters lay side by side. The familiar compass symbol stared back at him, almost mocking him with its simple elegance. His eyes narrowed as he examined the paper more closely.

The first letter had come in a simple envelope, the seal just a subtle mark of authority. But the second note was different. The paper was heavier, the ink darker, more deliberate. It felt older somehow—like a piece of a puzzle he had yet to understand.

What had Olivia meant when she said, *"Trust no one?"* The words still echoed in his mind. He reached for his phone again, dialing her number, but this time it went straight to voicemail. He left a brief message, though part of him knew it wouldn't change anything. Olivia had been more than just a friend over the years; she had been his anchor, but now she was slipping through his fingers.

What had she meant by *"they're watching"*?

As the minutes passed, the weight of the unknown grew. Elliot knew he couldn't wait any longer. Something was closing in on him, something he couldn't outrun. There was a choice he had to make, and it felt like it was a matter of life and death.

He walked back to the front door, his mind still spinning, his thoughts chasing each other in an endless circle. The apartment hallway stretched before him, empty and quiet, but he knew—he *knew*—that something was lurking just out of sight.

Another knock.

It was quicker this time—three fast raps that echoed in the stillness of the apartment. Elliot's heart jumped in his chest. He moved toward the door, trying to keep his breathing steady, but the anticipation was almost too much to bear.

He opened it. No one was there.

But there was something waiting for him—another note, just like the others, this one tucked carefully into the crack of the doorframe. Elliot reached down, his fingers trembling as he took it. He opened it slowly, careful not to tear the delicate paper.

The note read:

"Time is running out. Make your decision now, or it will be made for you. The clock is ticking, and you cannot stop it."

Elliot's throat went dry. His mind raced with all the possibilities, but none of them made any sense. What was the game here? Who was controlling it? And why him?

He looked around, his eyes scanning every corner of his apartment, his mind struggling to keep up with the surreal nature of it all. He couldn't do this alone anymore. He needed to find answers.

With the note clenched tightly in his hand, he turned toward the door, ready to step into the unknown. But before he could reach for the handle, a flash of movement caught his eye—a figure in the shadows, standing just beyond the streetlight, watching him.

His breath caught in his throat.

He wasn't alone anymore.

3

The Invisible Threads

The figure remained in the shadows, barely visible beneath the streetlight, its presence like a cold whisper against the still night. Elliot's heart hammered in his chest as he took a cautious step back, his mind racing, his instincts screaming for him to retreat. But the door was already open, and whatever was out there—whatever was pulling him into this mess—was waiting.

He stood frozen, his breath shallow, trying to make sense of the figure in the darkness. It was too far away for him to make out any details, but he could feel its gaze, sharp and intent. The hairs on the back of his neck stood on end. Whoever they were, they weren't here by chance.

Elliot's hand tightened around the door handle, the cool metal offering little comfort. His mind reeled back to the cryptic messages he'd received—the letters, the warnings, the phone call. Was this the moment everything had been building to? The weight of the decision he had yet to make?

Another figure appeared from the darkness, just as silent as the first. It was a woman, her face obscured by a dark scarf, but her posture was unmistakable—confident, sure. A third figure emerged, this one taller, with an air of authority that was impossible to ignore. He stepped forward, the others falling in line behind him, like pieces of a puzzle locking into place.

Elliot's throat went dry. He wanted to slam the door shut, to bolt and hide, but something—some unexplainable force—held him in place. He didn't know who they were or why they were here, but one thing was clear: they weren't here to ask questions. They were here to give orders.

He swallowed hard, his voice barely a whisper. "Who are you?"

The man in the front—the leader, perhaps—paused just short of the doorway. His eyes gleamed beneath the dim light, cold and calculating, as though he already knew Elliot's every move. "We're the ones who've been watching," he said, his voice low and smooth, like silk sliding across a blade. "And we've come to collect what's ours."

Elliot's heart skipped a beat. He didn't understand. What did they want from him? What was he supposed to have?

"Collect?" Elliot echoed, his voice sounding foreign even to him. "What the hell are you talking about?"

The woman stepped forward then, her eyes meeting his with a cold, unsettling calm. "The time for questions is over," she said. "You've made your choice. Now, you must face the consequences."

Elliot's blood ran cold. He wasn't sure whether he was speaking to enemies or people who held the key to something he needed to understand. His pulse raced as he glanced between the figures in front of him, their faces unreadable, their intentions unclear. He had only seconds to decide how to act, but he couldn't bring himself to move.

"Why me?" Elliot asked, his voice cracking as the weight of the situation pressed down on him. "What do you want from me?"

The leader stepped forward, his gaze unwavering. "It's not about what we want," he said, his voice cold and distant. "It's about what you're willing to sacrifice to keep your secrets safe."

The words hit Elliot like a slap to the face. His mind scrambled for answers, but the more he thought about it, the more he realized just how little he understood. What secrets? What was so important that these people— whoever they were—had been watching him?

"Secrets?" Elliot repeated, disbelief creeping into his voice. "I don't have any secrets. I'm just a guy trying to get through life."

The leader's lips curled into something that wasn't quite a smile. "You think that's all you are? Just another face in the crowd?" He took a step closer, his eyes narrowing. "You've been chosen, Elliot. And you've made your decision. But now you must live with it."

Elliot's legs felt like jelly, the weight of their words settling like an anchor in his stomach. He couldn't look away from the leader's eyes, though he didn't want to. He wanted to slam the door shut, to end this nightmare before it even began. But there was something about their presence that kept him rooted to the spot. Something that told him he had no choice but to face this head-on.

"What happens now?" Elliot asked, his voice barely above a whisper.

The leader smiled again, a predatory grin that sent a chill through Elliot's spine. "Now, you come with us. We have much to discuss, and we can't afford any more delays."

The woman stepped forward, her movements fluid and silent. Her hand reached into the folds of her coat, producing something small and metallic, glinting under the streetlight. She held it out to Elliot, her expression unreadable. It was a small key, ornate and delicate, with intricate designs carved into the surface.

Elliot's eyes locked on the key, the shape of it somehow familiar, though he couldn't place where he'd seen it before. The woman's voice cut through his thoughts, sharp and clear. "This key is your first step," she said. "But it comes with a price."

He looked back at her, the knot in his stomach tightening. "A price?"

She didn't respond, instead turning toward the street with a single, graceful motion of her hand. Without a word, the three figures began to walk away, their footsteps as soft as the night air. But the key remained in Elliot's hand, a weight that felt too heavy to bear.

He stood there for a moment, the cold air pressing in around him, as the figures disappeared into the shadows. His mind was spinning, his thoughts a blur of confusion and fear. What was going on? Who were they? And why had he been chosen?

The silence seemed to stretch on forever, the weight of the moment pressing on him with increasing force. He didn't know what to do, but he couldn't stand there any longer.

With a deep breath, Elliot stepped into the hallway, his hand still clutching the key. The night felt darker now, as if the very air around him had shifted. And as he walked deeper into the unknown, he could feel the invisible threads that had been tugging at him—guiding him, pulling him into something he had yet to understand—tightening their grip.

4

The Hollow Silence

The key felt impossibly cold in Elliot's hand as he walked through the empty streets, the faint echo of his footsteps the only sound in the stillness of the night. His mind raced with questions, each one more urgent than the last. Who were they? What did they want from him? And why had they chosen him?

The darkness around him seemed to stretch on forever, the faint glow of streetlights casting long shadows that twisted and curled like something alive. His heart beat erratically in his chest, but he couldn't stop moving. The key— the symbol of his involvement—was an anchor pulling him forward. Yet with every step, the weight of it grew heavier, as if the very air itself was beginning to push against him.

Ahead, a figure stood in the doorway of an old, decrepit building. The faint light of a nearby lamp flickered, casting the figure's silhouette in sharp relief. Elliot's breath caught in his throat as he approached. The figure did not move, but there was something familiar about the stance, the way they stood with a quiet authority that made the hairs on the back of his neck stand up.

He slowed his pace, every instinct telling him to turn and run, to leave this behind and never look back. But the thought of the key in his hand, the knowledge that whatever this was had already begun, kept him rooted to the ground. He had to know what this was about. He had to understand what was happening to him.

The figure shifted slightly, and Elliot froze. For a long moment, they simply stood there, the only movement the faint rustle of the wind against their coat. Finally, they spoke.

"Elliot," their voice was low, almost a whisper, but it carried a weight that made the air around them vibrate. "I've been waiting for you."

The words hung in the air, heavy and unsettling. Elliot's stomach twisted, and his pulse quickened. He didn't move, didn't speak, but inside, everything screamed for him to turn and run.

"I don't—" he started, but the figure raised a hand, silencing him.

"You don't have to say anything. You already know why you're here."

The voice was familiar, but there was something off about it. A coldness beneath the calm, as though the words were calculated, designed to stir something deep inside him. Something he didn't want to feel.

The figure stepped forward, their silhouette becoming clearer in the dim light. The coat they wore was long, dark, and flowing, almost like a shadow itself. They were tall, their presence commanding, and their eyes gleamed with an intensity that made Elliot feel like he was being measured, scrutinized.

Elliot didn't speak. He couldn't find the words, not with that feeling creeping up his spine, urging him to run, to get away. He glanced at the building behind the figure, its walls crumbling, windows boarded up. There was something ancient about it, something that made the hairs on the back of his neck prickle.

The figure took another step forward, their eyes locked onto his. "You've already crossed the threshold, Elliot. You can't go back now."

Elliot's breath caught in his throat. He didn't understand. What threshold? What had he crossed? He had been minding his own business just days ago, and now—now everything felt twisted, like reality itself was bending around him. He had to get answers.

"Tell me what's going on," Elliot demanded, his voice shaking, but stronger now, more determined. "What do you want from me?"

The figure's lips curled slightly into what might have been a smile. But it wasn't comforting. It wasn't warm. It was the kind of smile that sent shivers through him, the kind that made him feel like a pawn on a chessboard.

"It's not what we want from you, Elliot. It's what you need from us."

The words landed like a slap to his face. Need? What did he need from them? He didn't need anything. His life had been normal—mundane, even—and now it was anything but. Now, he was thrust into a world of shadows, of silent figures, of decisions he didn't remember making. He didn't need any of this.

"I don't need anything from you," he said, his voice steady, though his heart was racing. "I want you to leave me alone."

The figure's eyes darkened, their gaze sharpening. "It doesn't work like that," they said, their voice lowering. "You don't get to decide anymore. You're in this now, whether you want to be or not."

Elliot's breath hitched. The weight of their words settled around him, thick and suffocating. He didn't know what they were talking about. Didn't know what they meant by *being in this.*

The figure took a step back, motioning toward the building behind them. The door creaked open slowly, as if responding to the gesture. "Come inside, Elliot. It's time you understood."

Elliot stood frozen, staring at the open door. Everything in him screamed to refuse. To leave. To go back to his life, back to the normal, predictable existence he once knew. But the key... the key in his hand felt heavier now, more insistent, pulling him toward the door as though it held the answers to everything.

The figure stood silent, watching him, waiting. The air around them felt thick with expectation, as if the entire world had paused, holding its breath, waiting for him to make his choice. The building loomed like a sentinel, its broken windows watching, its doors open wide like the mouth of some ancient beast.

Elliot's pulse raced as he glanced once more at the figure. He opened his mouth to speak, but the words caught in his throat. He had no idea what was inside that building. No idea what awaited him behind that door. But he knew one thing—whatever it was, he was being drawn in, whether he liked it or not.

And then, as if a switch had been flipped, the decision was made. He stepped forward, his feet moving of their own accord. The cold air bit into his skin as he walked, but he didn't stop. The door closed behind him with a soft, ominous thud, and he was swallowed by the darkness.

Inside, the silence was hollow, stretching out like an empty cavern, waiting to be filled. The figure had already disappeared into the shadows, but Elliot could feel their presence, like a weight pressing down on him. He had crossed the threshold. He had made his choice.

Now, there was no turning back.

5

The Unseen Path

Elliot's steps echoed through the vast, empty hall, each footfall reverberating against the cold stone walls. The air was thick, heavy with a silence that felt almost alive, pressing in on him from all sides. His breath came in shallow bursts, his heartbeat loud in his ears. The darkness seemed to stretch endlessly, swallowing everything in its path, yet just beyond his reach, faint outlines of shapes loomed in the shadows. It was as though the building itself were holding its breath, waiting for him to make the next move.

His fingers tightened around the key in his pocket, the metal digging into his skin through the fabric. He had no idea where he was going, or why he was still moving forward. The rational part of his brain screamed at him to turn back, to run. But the deeper, quieter voice inside him urged him onward, whispering that this was what he had to do.

"Where am I?" His voice sounded small, lost in the vast emptiness.

There was no reply, only the soft creaking of the building as if it were shifting, settling, and a faint hum that seemed to vibrate beneath his feet. A low thrum that almost seemed like a heartbeat. The strange sensation crawled up his spine, making his skin prickle, but he couldn't pinpoint where it was coming from, or what it meant.

He kept walking.

As he moved deeper into the building, the shadows grew thicker. It was impossible to tell whether the darkness was the result of the absence of light, or something else—something darker, something more deliberate. Every few steps, he glanced over his shoulder, half-expecting to see something—or someone—looming in the space he had just passed. But the hall remained empty.

He stopped in front of a large, ornately carved door, the only one in the hall with visible markings—strange symbols etched into the wood, symbols that seemed to shimmer slightly as though they were alive. He could feel the pull toward it, a magnetic force that tugged at him, urging him closer.

Before he could reach for the handle, a voice broke the silence.

"You shouldn't be here."

The voice was low, familiar, but not comforting. It was cold, distant, like the wind through the cracks of a forgotten place.

Elliot spun around, his heart thundering in his chest. But there was nothing behind him—nothing except the empty, oppressive darkness.

"You can't run away from it, Elliot," the voice continued, now much clearer, as though it were inside his head rather than coming from the air around him. "It's already started."

The blood drained from his face, his body going cold. He didn't recognize the voice, but there was something about it that felt personal, like it knew him—knew his thoughts, his fears.

"I'm not running," Elliot replied, his voice shaking despite his efforts to sound steady. "What do you want from me?"

The only response was the faintest shift in the air, a sound like fabric rustling, but when Elliot turned to look, there was nothing. He felt the weight of the silence crushing in on him, the quiet pressing so heavily that it almost felt suffocating. He was alone. Or at least, he thought he was.

The key in his pocket felt warmer now, its jagged edges pressing against his thigh as if it were alive, urging him forward. He turned back to the door, his hand reaching for the ornate handle. He hesitated just for a moment, the weight of the decision settling over him. Should he open it? What lay behind it?

His hand closed around the handle, and with a deep breath, he twisted it.

The door opened with a low, groaning creak, revealing a room bathed in shadow. There were no lights, no candles. Only an oppressive, unnatural darkness. It seemed to pulse with a life of its own.

Elliot took a step inside, his heart racing. The air grew heavier, thick with a sense of expectation. He could feel something watching him, not from a distance, but from within the darkness itself. He could sense its presence, cold and suffocating, pressing in on him from all sides.

The door slammed shut behind him, the sound so sudden, so violent, that it made him jump. His breath caught in his throat. He was trapped.

"Hello?" His voice cracked in the silence. No response.

He tried to move, but the air seemed thicker now, almost like he was wading through water. Every step felt like it took more effort than it should. The weight in his chest grew, and a faint, unsettling sound began to grow from the darkness, a soft scraping noise like nails against stone, slow, deliberate.

Elliot turned in place, but the room seemed to stretch and shift, the walls closing in on him, making it impossible to find the edges. There were no windows, no escape routes. The room was an abyss.

The scraping sound grew louder. Closer. His breath caught in his throat as he spun around, his eyes desperately scanning the shadows.

Suddenly, the sound stopped.

"Who's there?" His voice was barely a whisper now, fear curling in his gut.

And then—nothing.

For a moment, the silence returned, but now it felt different. He could feel it pressing against his skin, suffocating, like the weight of a thousand unspoken thoughts, of something looming, waiting.

Something was coming.

Out of the corner of his eye, he saw it—a flicker of movement in the darkness, something shifting, something not quite human. His heart pounded in his chest, and he took a step back, stumbling over his own feet. His head whipped around, but there was nothing there. Nothing but the shadows that seemed to move with an unnatural life of their own.

The scraping sound returned, this time more erratic, more frantic, as if whatever it was had realized he had seen it.

Without thinking, Elliot turned and ran. The room stretched before him, endlessly long, the walls closing in like they were coming to crush him. His legs burned, his breath ragged as he ran through the heavy darkness, but no matter how fast he moved, the door, the way out, was always just out of reach.

His pulse raced. Sweat beaded on his forehead.

Something was behind him, following him. It was too close. He could feel its presence, like a shadow clinging to his skin, creeping up his back, its cold breath on the back of his neck.

Desperation surged through him. He had to get out.

He didn't dare look back, but he felt it, heard it—the scrape, the dragging sound. It was so close now, close enough that he could almost feel it reaching for him.

With one final burst of energy, he lunged forward, crashing into the door. It flew open, the light of the hallway pouring in like a beacon. He didn't look back as he scrambled into the hall, the darkness of the room swallowed by the light.

The door slammed shut behind him, the scraping sound gone, replaced by the relentless thrum of his heartbeat. He stood there, gasping for air, his mind racing, trying to process what had just happened.

What was that thing? What was it trying to do to him?

And more importantly, why had it been waiting for him?

6

Echoes of the Past

The moment Elliot stepped out of the shadowed hall, the oppressive weight that had suffocated him inside seemed to lift, but only slightly. His breath still came in short, panicked gasps, his eyes darting to every corner, as if the darkness would suddenly reclaim him. But the hall beyond the door was quiet—unnervingly so. The usual hum of the building was absent, replaced by a vacuum of silence that felt heavier than the room he had just escaped from.

He stood there, eyes locked on the door behind him, heart thudding in his chest. His mind raced through the fragments of the experience—the shifting darkness, the scraping sound, the feeling that something had been watching him, waiting for him. He could still hear that scraping, that dragging, like nails on stone, faint but real in the recesses of his mind. It didn't feel like something he could easily shake off.

He backed away from the door slowly, his body instinctively seeking distance from whatever had lurked behind it. The hallway ahead of him seemed ordinary—too ordinary, in fact. The same stone walls, the same flickering overhead lights that barely illuminated the way. But something about the hallway felt wrong now, like it had changed, or rather, like it was no longer the place he had thought it was.

The sound of footsteps echoed in the distance—slow, deliberate, and oddly in tune with the rhythm of his heart. Elliot froze. The footsteps weren't his. They weren't anyone's in the building, as far as he knew. He had been alone.

He strained his ears, trying to determine the source of the noise. His body tensed, every muscle coiled, ready to spring into action. The footsteps grew louder, drawing closer, and then—just as quickly—paused. Silence.

Elliot's gaze snapped to the far end of the hallway, where the light seemed to flicker just a little more urgently than before. His body screamed at him to run, to get out of the building before whatever was stalking him found him, but his legs felt like lead. The key in his pocket burned through the fabric, its weight a constant reminder of why he was here.

With each step he took, the tension in the air thickened, a static charge he could almost taste. He reached for the key, fingers brushing against the cold metal, pulling it out just to feel the sense of purpose it gave him. At the end of the hall was a door, almost identical to the others, but there was something about it that called to him. He didn't know why, but he had to go there.

The footsteps started again, this time faster, closer—whoever or whatever was moving through the halls, it was now following him. Elliot glanced back, his pulse spiking as the distant shadows along the walls seemed to stretch toward him, creeping like fingers trying to grab hold of him.

It was only when he reached the door that the sound of footsteps stopped. The silence, however, was deafening. The air was still, almost unnaturally so.

He hesitated, hand trembling as it hovered over the door handle. In the quiet, he could almost hear his heartbeat in his ears, a rhythmic thudding that only heightened the tension. He knew he couldn't stay here, but what lay beyond the door?

There was only one way to find out.

His hand gripped the handle, turning it slowly, and the door opened with a soft creak. Elliot stepped inside.

The room was larger than he had expected. The walls were lined with old shelves, most of them empty, save for a few dusty books scattered haphazardly across the floor. There was a strange, almost familiar smell in the air— something old, musty, and a little metallic.

The room seemed to stretch before him, and as his eyes adjusted to the dim light, he noticed something that made his blood run cold. On the far side of the room was a large, ornate mirror—its surface cracked and discolored, yet still intact. In front of it stood a figure.

The figure was blurry at first, like a smear in the reflection. But as Elliot stepped forward, it became clearer—too clear. A woman, her face pale and gaunt, her long dark hair falling around her face like a curtain. She was staring at him through the mirror, her lips parted slightly as though she were about to speak, but no words came.

Elliot felt his breath catch in his throat. He had seen her before—he was sure of it—but where? He couldn't place it. His heart began to race, his pulse quickening as he took another step forward.

The woman's reflection shifted suddenly. It was subtle, almost imperceptible, but something in her movements was wrong. She reached up with one hand, and for a moment, Elliot thought she was going to touch the glass. But then, her fingers curled into a fist, and the air seemed to grow cold.

Elliot stepped back instinctively, bumping into one of the shelves. The sound was deafening in the quiet, the books falling to the floor with a sharp clatter.

The woman's reflection jerked in response, her head snapping toward him, her eyes wide with an intensity that felt almost painful. And then, the most chilling thing happened—her lips began to move.

But no sound came.

Her eyes locked onto his, and for a brief moment, Elliot felt a strange sensation—a pull, like a gravity that was not his own. He reached forward instinctively, drawn to her, but just as his fingers brushed the edge of the mirror, a loud bang echoed through the room.

The door slammed shut behind him, and the woman in the mirror let out a sound—an awful, strangled sound that vibrated through the walls. Elliot stumbled back, his breath ragged, his mind scrambling for logic. The mirror's surface rippled like water, and for a moment, it seemed as though the woman might step out of the reflection and into the room with him.

He spun toward the door, but it wouldn't open. He tugged at the handle desperately, but it was as if the door had fused with the frame. The silence returned, suffocating, pressing in on him. He was trapped.

And then, in the corner of his vision, something moved. A shadow, fleeting but unmistakable.

A whisper.

It wasn't a voice, not in the way he understood voices. But it was there—soft, like a breath against his ear.

"You shouldn't have come."

7

The Hollow Sound

The walls of the room seemed to close in on Elliot as his breath caught in his chest. He tugged once more at the door, panic rising like an insistent tide. The handle didn't budge. A faint echo of the whisper still lingered in the air, a low, cold murmur that sent a chill down his spine. "You shouldn't have come."

He could hear the rhythmic beat of his pulse, each thud reverberating in his skull, drowning out everything else. His fingers trembled, slick with sweat as they gripped the door handle once more, twisting in desperation. But the metal was unforgiving, an immovable force.

Behind him, the cracked mirror shimmered in the half-light. The reflection of the woman, her face pale and haunting, had not shifted from her stance. She stood perfectly still, her black eyes locked onto his, and for a moment, Elliot could have sworn her lips were moving, forming words that he could not hear.

A sudden thud from the other side of the room pulled him from his trance. His heart raced, pounding in his ears, as he whipped his head around, searching the dim corners. The noise hadn't come from the mirror; it had come from the shelves—no, the walls themselves. He stepped back cautiously, his feet brushing against the scattered books, the only sound in the room now the sharp rasp of his breathing.

Something was wrong. Everything felt wrong.

Elliot's mind raced, struggling to make sense of the situation. The door wouldn't open. The mirror held the woman's reflection, her lifeless gaze never wavering. The room felt alive in some strange, unnerving way, as if it were breathing, pulsing with a force beyond his understanding.

Another thud.

This time, it was louder, more insistent. He turned toward the source of the noise, his eyes scanning the shelves. Nothing had changed—except for the stillness that clung to every object in the room, like a waiting predator.

He took a slow step toward the corner, his every instinct screaming at him to leave, to run, but his legs felt like lead. The door was still useless, the mirror still contained the figure that seemed to be watching him. The woman's expression had changed—her face was now filled with an almost malicious glee, her lips curling into a smile that didn't belong to someone alive.

The thud came again, louder this time, as if it were a knock. Elliot froze, eyes darting from the shelves to the walls, to the mirror.

The floor creaked beneath him.

Without thinking, Elliot reached for one of the books that had fallen from the shelves. He grabbed it by the spine and held it out like a weapon, a pitiful defense against whatever was waiting for him in the shadows. But as his fingers closed around the book, he realized that it was heavier than it should have been, like it had absorbed something—something dark, something wrong.

And then, the knocking came again.

This time, it wasn't from the walls—it was from the mirror.

Elliot's breath hitched in his throat as his eyes shot toward the reflection. The woman in the mirror was now moving, her hand rising, her fingers pressed flat against the glass. And with each knock that echoed from the other side of the room, the glass rippled, as if it were liquid. The reflection of the woman began to distort, the once-perfect image of her face warping into something far darker, a grotesque twist of features that made Elliot's stomach churn.

Thud. Thud. Thud.

Each knock became faster, louder, more insistent, until the entire mirror seemed to vibrate with the force of it. The room itself trembled in response. The glass rippled like water disturbed by a stone, distorting the woman's form until she was no longer recognizable. Her body contorted unnaturally, her arms stretching impossibly long, fingers elongating to reach toward the edges of the frame. Her eyes—those cold, dead eyes—now seemed to pierce through the mirror and lock onto Elliot, as if she were reaching out to him.

Elliot's hand shot out, and he slammed the book into the mirror. The impact made no sound, and the book passed through the glass as though it were smoke, dissipating into the air.

He stepped back, chest heaving, eyes wide with terror, but there was nowhere to go. No escape. The knocking stopped. The room went still again. But now, in the space where the mirror had once been, there was only a jagged outline, a crack splitting the surface like a wound.

The walls of the room seemed to breathe, in and out, slowly, rhythmically, as if they were alive. The air felt thick, suffocating, and each breath Elliot took seemed harder than the last.

A low, guttural sound vibrated from deep within the walls.

A voice.

It was muffled, distant, but unmistakable. Words. Choked, gasping words. He couldn't understand them, but they were there.

"Elliot..."

He froze. His name.

The voice, though faint, was unmistakable.

"Elliot... come closer."

It was soft, almost pleading. He swallowed, his throat dry, his hands shaking as they pressed against the cold walls for support. A hundred thoughts whirled in his mind, each one more terrifying than the last. His feet moved of their own accord, despite the instinct to run, to escape. He could not resist.

"Come closer, Elliot," the voice whispered again, more insistent this time.

He stepped forward, barely able to breathe. Each step felt like it weighed a hundred pounds, the air thickening, the walls closing in even further. The crack in the mirror was now large enough to allow a faint, flickering light to seep through, and Elliot reached out toward it, fingers trembling. As he touched the surface, the warmth of the light flooded his skin, spreading up his arm like fire.

And then, the world went black.

He heard a sound—a deep, resonant hum that vibrated in his bones. When his vision returned, he was no longer in the room. He was somewhere else. Somewhere darker. The voice echoed in his mind.

"You shouldn't have come…"

8

The Weight of Shadows

The first thing Elliot noticed was the silence. It wasn't the kind of silence that felt comforting or peaceful. It was heavy. Dense. The kind of silence that presses down on you until you feel as if the air itself is thick enough to suffocate. The darkness surrounding him was absolute. No light. No sounds. Just the suffocating stillness that clung to his skin, as though the very atmosphere were trying to pull him into itself, to swallow him whole.

He took a deep breath, but it tasted like ash, dry and bitter. His chest tightened, and he instinctively brought a hand up to rub his throat. The air wasn't just thick—it was oppressive, as if every breath he took was an effort against some unseen force.

"Where am I?" His voice was a whisper, swallowed by the blackness.

He had no answer.

He reached out, his hands feeling through the void. His fingers brushed against something cold, smooth, metallic. The chill of it seemed to seep through his skin, sending a shiver down his spine. His heart skipped in his chest. What was it? He couldn't see it. Couldn't hear anything except his own shallow breath, racing in the dark.

He fumbled forward, his palms grazing more of the cold, unfamiliar surface.

It felt like the walls were closing in, the space shrinking around him. No matter which direction he turned, his hands always met the same cold metal, smooth and unyielding. The walls pressed closer, and the shadows twisted like living things, swirling around him with an intelligence that made his skin crawl.

Elliot stepped back, his foot brushing against something sharp, jagged. He hissed in pain as a shard of something broke against his heel, its sharp edges cutting into his skin. Blood welled up, hot and dark, staining the ground beneath him. He took another step back, hoping to find something, anything that could help him, but there was nothing.

"Help..." His voice trembled, but it too was swallowed by the shadows. He looked down at his foot, the blood pooling around his ankle, and it was then he noticed something strange. The blood was spreading—not just across the floor—but along the walls. It was as if the shadows themselves were drawing it in, feeding off the very life he was losing.

His heart hammered in his chest. "No... no, no, no!"

He tried to step away, but the darkness was everywhere. It wasn't just surrounding him anymore—it was inside him. He could feel it, thick and cold, crawling through his veins, wrapping around his bones. His pulse quickened, the pressure inside his chest rising until he thought he might suffocate. It was like something was squeezing him from the inside out.

A low hum began to reverberate from deep within the darkness. It started as a low murmur, something almost imperceptible, and then it grew, louder and louder, until it vibrated through his bones. His legs buckled beneath him as the sound surged like a wave crashing through him. It was too much. Too much.

His body screamed for him to move, to flee, but his limbs were locked in place, frozen by the crushing weight of the shadows that now seemed to be pulling him toward the center of the room. Or maybe it was pulling him toward something else.

A flicker of light appeared out of nowhere, faint and weak, but enough to cut through the overwhelming blackness. It was a figure, standing in the center of the room, illuminated by the flickering light. It wasn't a person—at least, not fully. The figure was human, but its shape shifted with every blink, its form warping like liquid, swirling in and out of focus. One moment it was tall, with elongated limbs, and the next, it was a hunched figure, its face a blur of sharp angles and shadows.

Elliot's breath caught in his throat as the figure reached out, its fingers impossibly long, stretching toward him. The touch was like ice, cold enough to freeze his skin, and when it wrapped around his arm, a jolt of pain shot through him. He gasped, but no sound came out. His mouth was dry, his throat constricted, and the darkness seemed to press in harder, deeper.

He tried to pull away, but the figure's grip tightened. His skin burned where it touched him, the searing cold leaving behind a trail of frost. The shadows around them seemed to pulse in time with the figure's movements, a rhythm that thrummed through the air like a heartbeat.

And then the voice came again.

"You shouldn't have come."

The words were like a whip, cracking in the stillness, each syllable laced with venom. The figure leaned closer, its face—if it could be called that—coming into sharper focus. It was twisted, broken, its features melting together, as though it had been stitched together from the remnants of other faces, other people.

Elliot's pulse raced, panic flooding him as he struggled to break free. His feet slid beneath him, his blood now dripping freely from his foot, leaving a trail behind him as he moved. The figure's grip remained unyielding, its cold fingers like iron clamps.

"You don't belong here," the voice rasped again, a sound like broken glass. "And you won't leave."

He opened his mouth to scream, but no sound came out. The figure's eyes— black pits of nothingness—locked onto his, and in that moment, Elliot knew.

There was no escape.

The figure's lips twisted into a grotesque smile, its expression shifting, elongating until it seemed to consume the whole of its face. And then, just as suddenly as it had appeared, it released him, pushing him backward with a force so strong it left him reeling.

Elliot's back slammed against the cold, unyielding wall, and the air rushed from his lungs. He gasped for breath, but it was as if the very atmosphere had turned to stone. Every inch of him screamed for release, for freedom from this suffocating nightmare, but there was nowhere to go.

The shadows continued to shift and pulse around him, their movements like whispers, like fingers sliding across his skin. The figure stood before him, its form now solidifying into something more human, its face now locked in a twisted grin that made his skin crawl.

"You've already chosen," the figure said, its voice a hollow echo that seemed to fill the room. "And now, there's no turning back."

Elliot's world fractured in that moment. His eyes blurred. His vision spun. And the last thing he saw before everything went dark was the figure's outstretched hand, reaching toward him with the promise of something far worse than death.

And then, nothing.

9

The Hollow Echo

The cold seeped into Rhea's bones, numbing her fingers and tightening the skin around her joints. The hallway stretched before her like an endless corridor, its walls narrowing with each step she took. She had lost track of time; how long had it been since she first stepped into this place? An hour? A day? There was no way to know. The darkness that swallowed her surroundings made every moment feel both stretched and compressed, as if time itself was playing tricks on her.

Rhea's heart pounded in her chest, the steady thrum of it like a drumbeat, echoing in her ears. She hadn't meant to come here. No, she hadn't wanted this. She never asked for any of this. But now that she was here, there was no turning back. The air around her felt wrong—like it was made of something other than air. The faint buzzing in her head made it impossible to focus. It was as if the very walls themselves were alive, breathing, watching her.

Her breath was shallow, her legs unsteady beneath her. The flickering lights above cast long, sharp shadows, which danced across the walls, twisting into monstrous shapes. She clenched her fists, the edges of her nails digging into her palm as she tried to maintain some semblance of control.

Every now and then, she could hear it—the faint echo of a sound that seemed to reverberate from deep within the walls. A soft tapping, a scraping, or was it something else? Her mind struggled to make sense of it. Was it a footstep? Or something far worse?

Her senses were on high alert as she moved forward, the silence that had once comforted her now suffocating, filling her lungs with the scent of damp, decaying wood. She glanced over her shoulder once, but all she saw was the shadowed path she had just crossed. Nothing was behind her. Not yet. But something was coming. She could feel it in the air. It was there, just out of sight, but undeniably present. A chill ran down her spine, making the hairs on the back of her neck stand up.

Another echo.

A scraping sound.

Closer this time.

Rhea spun around, her hand instinctively reaching for the flashlight in her pocket. Her fingers brushed against it, but before she could pull it out, the light flickered—then died completely. The darkness felt absolute, impenetrable.

Her breath quickened as her eyes strained to see in the absence of light, but it was no use. The blackness had a weight to it, pressing in from every side. Her pulse raced, her heart pounding so loudly that it drowned out every other sound. She felt the walls closing in, the very floor beneath her feet seeming to shift.

Then came the whisper. Soft at first, but growing louder with each passing second. Rhea froze, her entire body tense as the voice slithered through the air like a snake. It was faint, barely audible at first, but it was unmistakable.

"You shouldn't be here."

Rhea's blood ran cold. The voice was familiar, but she couldn't place it. It was distant, detached, yet unmistakably real. The hairs on her arms stood at attention, the whisper seeping into her thoughts, worming its way through the cracks in her mind. She couldn't shake the feeling that it was watching her, waiting for her to make the wrong move.

"Go," the voice urged again, its tone colder now, sharper, more insistent. "Leave before it's too late."

But Rhea wasn't sure where "leave" even meant. There was no clear path to the exit. The hallway stretched endlessly, and every time she turned a corner, it felt like she was walking in circles. The weight in her chest grew heavier, suffocating. She needed to get out. She needed to escape. But the deeper she went, the more the darkness seemed to reach for her.

The whisper came again, this time closer, too close. It was as though it was right behind her, its breath hot against her ear. "You're too late," it hissed.

Rhea spun around in a panic, her eyes darting to the empty space behind her. But there was nothing—no figure, no form—just the oppressive darkness, the silence pressing in around her. Yet the voice remained, wrapping around her like a chain. Her pulse thundered in her ears as her mind raced to comprehend what was happening.

Suddenly, a sound broke the silence—a screech, a sharp, agonizing noise that sliced through the air like metal on stone. Rhea's body jerked in response, her feet moving before she even realized it. She couldn't stay here. Not for another second.

She bolted down the hallway, her footsteps echoing off the walls, the thud of each one reverberating in her chest. The air was thick with an unnatural stillness, but the presence behind her was undeniable now. She didn't have to look back to know it was there, following her every step, inching closer with each passing second.

Her vision blurred with the rush of panic. The hallway seemed to stretch further, twisting and curving in on itself. There was no escape. No exit.

And then, just as quickly as it had appeared, the floor beneath her feet gave way.

Rhea's heart lurched as the ground disappeared from under her, sending her plummeting into a dark abyss. Her stomach lurched in her throat as the world spun around her. She gasped, but the air was too thin. The fall felt endless, like she was falling into nothingness, swallowed by the void.

But then, without warning, she landed with a sickening thud, the impact rattling her bones. Pain exploded in her side, and for a moment, she couldn't breathe. She gasped, choking on the air, her chest constricting as if the very atmosphere was rejecting her presence.

Slowly, she pushed herself to her hands and knees, her breath ragged. Her eyes darted around, but there was nothing here either. No walls. No light. Just the oppressive silence and the weight of the shadows pressing down on her.

The voice was gone.

But Rhea knew one thing for sure: whatever this place was, it wasn't empty. And it wasn't finished with her yet.

The darkness shifted, and she felt the weight of a thousand eyes upon her, watching, waiting. There was no escape. She was trapped.

And whatever was coming for her, it was already here.

10

Beneath the Surface

Rhea's fingers scraped against the cold, jagged floor beneath her, her palms stinging from the rough texture of stone. She took shallow breaths, each one more labored than the last as she tried to steady her mind. The fall had left her disoriented, her vision clouded as she stared into the abyss around her. The blackness pressed in from all sides, swallowing her whole, yet she could feel something shifting—something alive in the dark.

Her heart pounded, each beat a drum that echoed in the silence. The emptiness stretched far beyond what she could see, but there was an unmistakable sensation in the air, a subtle vibration that hummed at the edge of her senses. She wasn't alone. She knew that much. But what was it? What had followed her down into this pit?

She pushed herself to her feet, every muscle in her body aching from the fall. The ground beneath her was unstable, shifting as though it were alive, pulsing with energy. It was as if the entire place was breathing, reacting to her presence. She could hear it now—faint, but undeniable: a soft, rhythmic thrumming, like the distant beat of a heart.

Rhea's eyes darted around, trying to adjust to the pitch-black surroundings, but it was no use. The darkness here was absolute. There were no stars, no shapes to form her bearings. No flicker of light.

A cold, bone-chilling wind swept past her, sending a shiver down her spine. She instinctively wrapped her arms around herself for warmth, but it did little to stop the creeping sensation of dread that crawled up her neck. She had to move. She had to get out of this place before whatever was lurking in the shadows found her. But where? Where was the way out?

The thrumming sound grew louder, closer. Rhea instinctively took a step back, her foot catching on something hard, sending her stumbling forward. She caught herself just before falling, her hand reaching out for something—anything—to steady her.

Her fingers brushed against a cold, metallic surface. It was smooth, slick to the touch, but strangely warm. She pressed her palm against it, trying to gauge its size, its shape. It felt like a wall, but it was different. Like something unnatural, something that didn't belong in this place.

The sound of the thrumming intensified, almost as if it were reacting to her touch. The ground beneath her feet trembled, and she could feel the air vibrating, like the building blocks of reality itself were shifting.

Suddenly, the surface before her split open with a low, ominous groan, and from the black void inside it, something reached out. Rhea gasped, stumbling backward as a thin, twisted tendril of shadow coiled its way into the air, reaching for her with unnatural speed.

Her pulse raced as her breath caught in her throat. She instinctively stumbled away, her legs unsteady as she tried to back away from the creeping darkness. But the tendril followed, winding toward her like a serpent. Its touch was cold, too cold. It felt wrong—unnatural—and Rhea could feel it pulling at something deep inside her, like it was trying to draw her into the heart of the darkness.

Her heart thudded painfully in her chest as she turned and fled, her feet pounding against the unstable ground. She couldn't look back. She couldn't afford to. But she could feel it chasing her. Could hear it slithering through the dark like a living thing, its tendrils scratching the stone behind her, getting closer with each step.

The ground beneath her feet seemed to change with every stride. She felt like she was running in circles, the air thick with the scent of damp earth and decay. The shadows were closing in, narrowing the path ahead, and her mind raced, trying to find an escape. But there was nowhere to run. This place—it had no exit, no end.

The walls of darkness seemed to pulse, contracting and expanding in time with the thrum of whatever was alive in the deep. The lightless expanse pressed against her like a physical force, suffocating her with each step she took.

She had to stop. She had to think.

Rhea stumbled to a halt, her breath ragged, her chest aching with exertion. She pressed her back against the nearest stone wall, trying to steady herself, to quiet the wild panic that clawed at the edges of her mind. The tendril was gone for now, but she could feel it. It was still there, watching her from the shadows.

The whisper returned then, softer than before, but with an unmistakable urgency. "You have to leave. Now."

Rhea's heart skipped a beat. The voice was familiar, but distant. She could hear it in the back of her mind, just beyond her reach. It wasn't human. It couldn't be. The words didn't make sense, didn't fit together as they should have. They were disjointed, like broken fragments of a thought, and yet, they had weight to them. Like they carried some hidden meaning, a warning she couldn't decipher.

The thrumming, the pulsing sound in the air, grew louder once more, vibrating through her bones, shaking her to her core. She felt her skin crawl. Something was coming, and this time, it wasn't just an echo in the dark. The shadows themselves were alive, reaching for her.

She couldn't wait. The walls were closing in.

Rhea turned and bolted forward again, pushing herself faster than before, adrenaline coursing through her veins. But as she ran, the very ground seemed to break apart beneath her. She slid down a slope, her legs slipping beneath her, and then, with a sickening lurch, she found herself tumbling into a deeper abyss. The air rushed out of her lungs, and for a moment, she thought she was falling again.

But then, the ground beneath her seemed to solidify. She crashed into something soft, yet firm—something that felt like flesh, but... wrong. The whisper in her mind echoed again, louder now, screaming at her to get up, to run.

But she didn't move.

Instead, she looked down, her breath caught in her throat.

The thing beneath her was alive. And it was staring back at her.

It wasn't human.

It wasn't anything she had ever seen before.

And it was waiting for her to make the next move.

A single, sharp tendril shot from the creature's form, reaching toward her like a snake. Rhea froze, the weight of its presence bearing down on her. The shadows around her twisted and bent in impossible shapes, and for the first time since she had fallen, Rhea understood one undeniable truth.

There was no way out. Not anymore.

Whatever was beneath the surface, whatever was waiting for her, had found her.

And it wasn't going to let her go.

11

The Edge of Silence

Rhea's heartbeat was the only sound in the darkness, thudding erratically in her ears as she lay motionless, the air heavy with something unnatural. Her hand still hovered near the shifting mass beneath her, its pulse slow and steady, as though waiting for her to make a choice. Her mind raced, the whispers in her mind—urgent, frantic—pushing her toward one single, undeniable truth. There was no way out.

But there had to be. There had to be something she could do.

She closed her eyes, squeezing them tight as she forced herself to slow her breathing, trying to tune out the creeping sensation of the tendril—still poised and waiting just inches from her—like a snake ready to strike. She could feel it now, more than ever before. This place wasn't just a physical trap. It was something deeper. Something older. A force more primal than anything she had ever known, and the creature beneath her... she didn't know what it was, but she felt it. It was waiting, like a predator, watching her every move, waiting for her to show fear.

It was intelligent.

Rhea clenched her jaw, trying to steady her nerves. There had to be a way out. There was always a way out.

But how? How could she even begin to fight something like this? She had no weapons, no allies—just the cold stone beneath her and the silence that pressed in from every angle. The tendril inched forward, its dark, inky surface slick and glistening. She couldn't see it clearly in the darkness, but she could feel it. The air hummed with its presence, as though it could sense her fear. Her pulse quickened.

Then, just as the tendril touched the edge of her skin, a low rumbling sound filled the air—deep and guttural, vibrating through the ground. Rhea's body went rigid at the sudden movement, her entire being screaming for her to run, but she couldn't. She couldn't move.

The rumbling stopped, and the silence that followed was even worse than the sound itself. It stretched out into the blackness, wrapping around her like a thick, suffocating blanket. Every part of her screamed to break free from the silence. But it was all-consuming. There was no escape. No sound. Nothing to fight.

And that was when it hit her—**the thing** beneath her didn't just feed on fear. It fed on **silence**.

The realization made her stomach lurch. Silence was its ally, its shield, its weapon. Every time she stood still, trying to think, trying to stay calm, she was feeding into its trap. The more she resisted, the more the silence deepened, until it swallowed her whole.

Her fingers twitched against the cold stone beneath her as the tendril drew back for a moment. The creature's presence loomed closer, but it didn't strike—not yet. Rhea's mind raced. There had to be a way to disrupt the silence, to break its hold on her.

And then, she remembered the whisper—**"You have to leave. Now."**

The voice hadn't been just an echo of thought. It had come from somewhere. Somewhere close.

Rhea's heart skipped a beat, her eyes snapping open. Could the whisper have been a warning from someone? Someone who had been here before? Someone who had survived?

The thought was fleeting, but the urgency stayed with her, pulling her in a direction she couldn't explain. She didn't have the luxury of time.

A low, shuddering hiss slid through the silence, snapping her attention back to the creature beneath her. The tendril was moving again, slower this time, as though it were savoring her hesitation.

Rhea's body tensed, and she willed herself to move, pushing off the stone beneath her. Every muscle screamed in protest, but she couldn't wait. She had to do something.

The darkness around her seemed to close in, tightening like a vice. The shadows stretched out, thin and clawed, wrapping around her as if they were alive. The ground under her feet began to shift again, the surface tilting beneath her. Something was coming. Something was about to break through the dark.

Without thinking, Rhea's hand shot forward, scraping along the ground, desperate to find anything—any kind of leverage, anything that could disrupt the stillness. Her fingers brushed against something hard and metallic—smooth, curved, but cold. She wrapped her hand around it instinctively, pulling it toward her.

It was a **door**—hidden beneath the layers of stone, a small, almost imperceptible gap that her fingers had just discovered. It was covered in a thin layer of dust and decay, but it was real. A way out.

Her pulse raced as she tested the door, pushing with all her might. But it didn't budge.

Another hiss came from the creature below, louder this time, and the shadows seemed to pulse with its anger, the very walls vibrating as though it were reacting to her movements. The air grew colder, and Rhea could feel the tendrils creeping back toward her, the darkness growing thicker.

She couldn't waste any more time.

Desperation flooded her chest, and with one last heave, she shoved harder. There was a groan—a deep, metallic screech that split the silence—and the door began to shift.

It opened.

A rush of air blasted out from the gap, carrying with it the scent of something ancient, something that didn't belong to this world. But the scent was familiar. It was like the smell of something forgotten, something sealed away for eternity.

Rhea didn't think twice. She shoved her body through the gap, feeling the weight of the world pressing down on her as the tendrils reached for her once more. But she was already through. She fell forward, crashing onto hard ground on the other side.

She gasped, rolling onto her back to catch her breath, her body heaving with effort. The air here felt different—less oppressive, but still thick with tension. She looked around, her eyes struggling to adjust to the faint light that seeped through cracks in the ceiling.

A dark shape loomed at the far end of the room, just beyond her reach. It was silent now—too silent. The rumbling had stopped, but she could still feel its presence.

It was watching her.

She had no idea where she was now. But there was no turning back.

The silence was still with her. It would never truly leave her.

And she had no idea how long she could keep running.

12

Beneath the Veil

Rhea's breath caught in her throat as the door creaked closed behind her, the sound more deafening than the crushing silence she had just escaped. She pressed her back against the cold stone wall, her hands trembling as they searched for something, anything, to steady herself. The room she found herself in was small—claustrophobic even. Her eyes, still adjusting to the dim light that flickered from unseen sources, scanned the room for a way forward, but all she saw were walls—smooth, uniform, and unyielding.

The air was dense, charged with a kind of pressure she couldn't explain. It wasn't just the weight of the room, nor the suffocating quiet that threatened to squeeze the life from her lungs. It was as though the very atmosphere had become a living thing, pressing in on her with every breath, every beat of her heart.

The faint sound of dripping water echoed somewhere in the distance, a solitary reminder that she wasn't alone in this place. It wasn't the comforting drip-drip of a leaky faucet—it was something far more ominous. The sound came and went, always lingering just out of reach, a constant pulse in the silence.

She could hear her pulse in her ears, too, like a drumbeat urging her to move. But where? How could she move in a place like this? She could barely even think, let alone act. The weight of the air was too much, too oppressive, dragging her thoughts into darker corners of her mind. And then, there was the whisper. Soft, so faint she almost thought she had imagined it, but it was there—a voice in the dark, just at the edge of her consciousness.

"Turn back."

The voice was low, almost pleading, but there was no one to be seen. The shadows danced across the walls, stretching and twisting in unnatural patterns. Rhea tried to shake off the chill that crept down her spine, but the air around her was like ice, seeping into her very bones. She could feel it—a presence, unseen yet palpable. It was waiting. Watching. And she knew, deep down, that she had made a terrible mistake.

She had come too far to turn back now.

She moved cautiously, her steps slow, deliberate. Every sound she made seemed to echo in the stillness, magnified, like the world was holding its breath in anticipation. As she walked, she noticed the walls weren't as smooth as they appeared at first. Faint scratches marred the stone, as if something—or someone—had clawed at it in desperation. Her fingers grazed the surface of the wall as she passed, and she shuddered at the coldness that seemed to radiate from it. It felt wrong, as though the very stone itself was alive, pulsing with some dark energy.

Ahead of her, the faintest glimmer caught her eye—a flicker of light, barely perceptible but undeniable. Her pulse quickened as she moved toward it, drawn to the light like a moth to a flame. The room narrowed as she walked, the space becoming more constricted, the walls closing in around her. She was almost there, almost to the light, when she stopped dead in her tracks.

The sound—so faint at first—grew louder. A rhythmic scraping, like nails dragging across stone, followed by a low, guttural growl that sent a wave of icy dread through her chest. She froze, her breath shallow, her mind racing for an explanation. There was something here with her. Something close.

Rhea's eyes darted around, desperately trying to pinpoint the source of the noise, but there was nothing—no movement, no figure emerging from the shadows. Just the sound, growing louder, closer. She felt it now, the air thickening, the oppressive weight becoming unbearable. The growl was now a low rumble, vibrating through the floor beneath her, like the growl of some massive beast waiting to strike.

Suddenly, the light ahead flared brighter, blinding her for a split second. She raised her hand instinctively to shield her eyes, but when she lowered it, the room had changed. The walls were no longer smooth and unyielding—they were warped, jagged, as though they had been bent and twisted by some unnatural force. The faint scratching sound was replaced by a shuffling, dragging noise, closer now, relentless.

Her heart pounded in her chest as she instinctively took a step back. Her mind screamed at her to run, to get out before whatever it was found her, but her legs wouldn't move. She was rooted to the spot, her body frozen with fear.

The growl grew louder, closer now, and Rhea finally turned, her eyes searching the room desperately. That's when she saw it.

A figure emerged from the shadows, tall and looming, a silhouette that seemed to merge with the darkness around it. Its movements were slow, deliberate, as if it were savoring her terror. Its eyes—if they could even be called eyes—glowed faintly in the dim light, a sickly yellow that sent a chill through her veins. She could feel its gaze on her, heavy and oppressive, like it was reading her very thoughts.

Her breath caught in her throat, her body trembling. The voice in her mind whispered again, this time louder, more insistent.

"Leave. Now. Before it's too late."

But Rhea couldn't move. She couldn't tear her eyes away from the creature, her body paralyzed with dread. The growl deepened, turning into a low hiss that rattled her bones, and the figure stepped forward.

A flash of movement. A sudden rush of wind. She didn't have time to think, to react. All she knew was that the creature was on her, its claws—long and jagged—reaching for her, its growl shaking the very air. She staggered backward, her heart pounding, but there was nowhere to go.

The walls pressed in, the air thick with the weight of fear and darkness. And in that moment, just as the creature's clawed hand reached for her, she heard it—the faintest whisper.

"Run."

The voice was different this time—urgent, frantic. It wasn't the same voice that had warned her before. No, this one was real, tangible. Someone else was here. Someone else who had been here before her.

Her legs moved before her mind could catch up, propelling her forward, away from the creature. The light ahead flickered, a promise of safety, of escape. Rhea ran toward it with all the strength she had left, the sound of the creature's pursuit echoing behind her. The growl was getting louder, closer, but she couldn't stop. Not now. Not when she was so close.

The light flared again, blinding her as she crossed the threshold.

And then everything went black.